Murray Unkovich

WILDLIFE

AUSTRALIA

First published in Australia in 2007 by Reed New Holland
an imprint of New Holland Publishers (Australia) Pty Ltd
Sydney • Auckland • London • Cape Town
1/66 Gibbes Street Chatswood NSW 2067 Australia
218 Lake Road Northcote Auckland New Zealand
86 Edgware Road London W2 2EA United Kingdom
80 McKenzie Street Cape Town 8001 South Africa

2 4 6 8 10 9 7 5 3 1

ISBN 9781741105858

Publisher: Martin Ford
Designer: Tania Gomes
Production: Linda Bottari
Printer: Everbest Printing Co., China

FRONT COVER: *Saltwater Crocodile.*

OPPOSITE: *An adult male Red-necked Pademelon.*

PICTURE CREDITS:

*theimagelibrary. com.au: front cover, pp. 2–3, 4–5, 19, 22, 23, 25r,
27, 35, 48,55, 58, 60, 61, 62, 63, 64, 68–69, 74, 75, 78, 80,
81, 84–85, 90, 91, 92–93, 94*

Lochman Transparencies: pp. 10–11

close-up-photolibrary.com: pp. 40, 41, 79

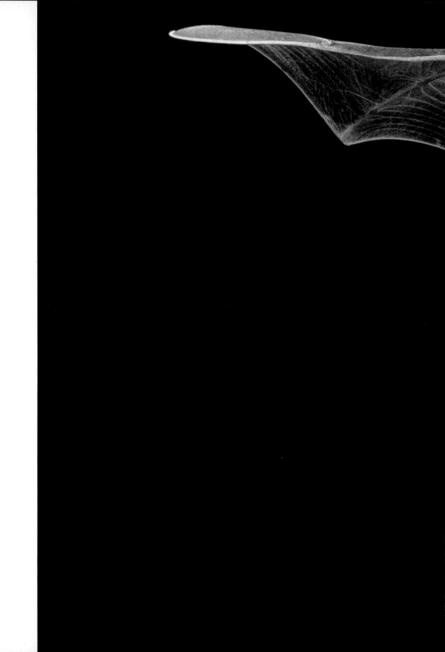

INTRODUCTION

Australia is blessed with a wonderful assortment of birds, mammals, reptiles, insects and other animals. They are all around you, in cities and urban areas, regional and national parks, and of course in the vast outback.

Wherever you travel you are sure to see conspicuous birds such as parrots and cockatoos, and of course kangaroos. However, if you pay attention you will see a myriad of other animals, from the somewhat drab to sparkling jewels.

I have been fortunate to have been able to travel to all Australian States and to witness some of Australia's vast collection of natural treasures. Some of these photographs have been taken in an instant, a fleeting glimpse stamped on to film. Others have taken many years to capture. Searching for a combination of rare animals, good light and a clear view can sometimes take a lifetime. In the meantime though, I have been able to photograph an assortment of unique subjects. I hope that through this, my first book, I am able to share some of the joy that these animals can bring.

RIGHT : *A Ghost Bat flies out to hunt at night. Ghost Bats are Australia's only carnivorous bats.*

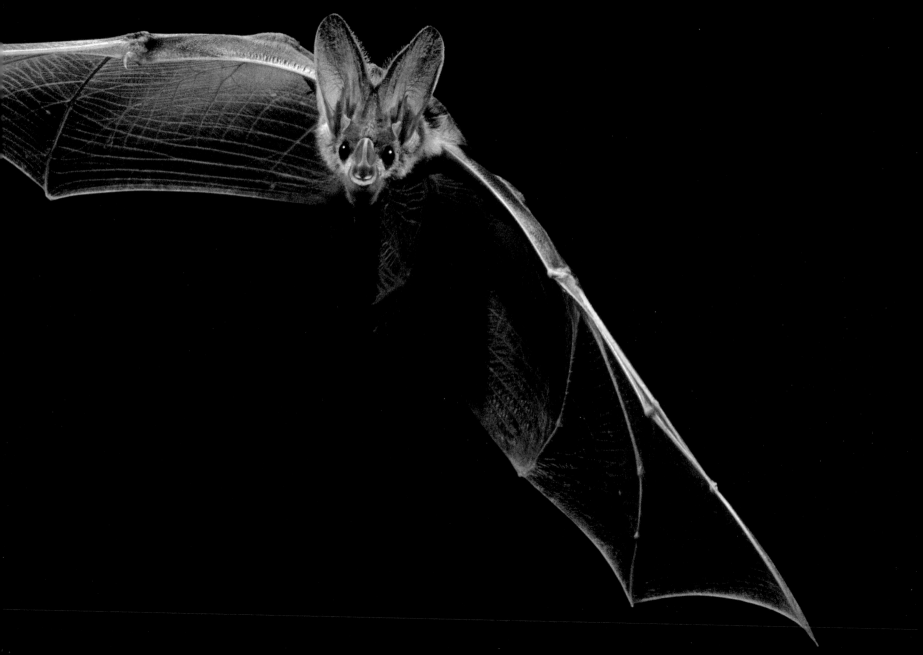

LEFT: *A Pacific Gull patrols the shoreline, Esperance, Western Australia.*
RIGHT: *Little Beach, Two Peoples Bay National Park, Western Australia.*

LEFT: *Tracks of the Gould's Monitor or Racehorse Goanna.*
ABOVE: *Standing to get a view above the reeds.*
RIGHT: *Gould's Monitor, a conspicuous lizard throughout sandy regions of Australia.*

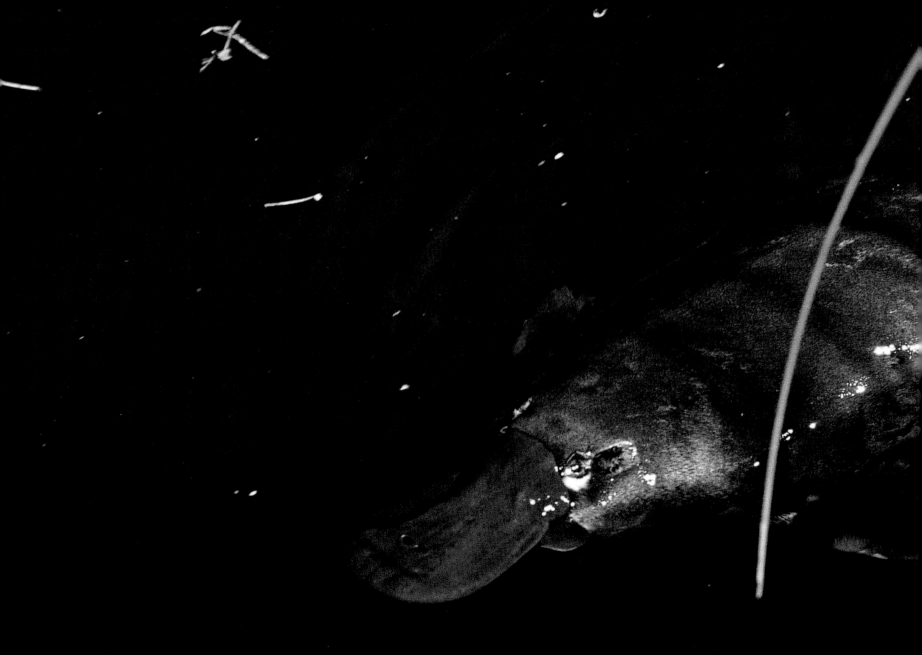

PREVIOUS PAGE: *A Platypus swims smoothly through quiet waters.*
LEFT: *A spider's net exposed in the early morning dew.*
RIGHT: *A squadron of Oleander Butterflies ready for take-off, Arnhem Land escarpment, Northern Territory.*

LEFT: *Lemon-flowered Gum.*
RIGHT: *A pair of Eastern Grey Kangaroos on Mt Ainslie, Canberra, overlooking Australia's Parliament House.*

LEFT: *Black Swans and young.*
RIGHT: *Cape Barren Geese sporting 'dayglo sunscreen', Tasmania.*

LEFT: *A paperbark swamp in the Western Australian wheatbelt.*
RIGHT: *Koala and young.*

PREVIOUS PAGE (LEFT): *Copland's Rock Frog lives in freshwater swamps near the south coast of Western Australia.*

PREVIOUS PAGE (RIGHT): *Major Mitchell or Pink Cockatoo, a beautiful but uncommon cockatoo of dry woodlands and deserts.*

LEFT: *Brushtail possums often live close to humans, even taking up residence in the roofs of houses.*

RIGHT: *Kookaburras are well known across Australia for their raucous laughing call.*

LEFT AND ABOVE: *Shell Beach in the Shark Bay World heritage area of Western Australia is made up of millions of small cockle shells that thrive in the bay's hypersaline water.*

RIGHT: *A dolphin at Monkey Mia, Shark Bay, Western Australia, where people and dolphins can often have close encounters.*

RIGHT: *The Tasmanian Devil, although shy, is a ferocious carnivore.*

LEFT: *A Great Egret, found in all types of waterbodies thoughout Australia, awaits its next meal.*

RIGHT: *The Straw-necked Ibis is also known as the 'farmers' friend' as it eats grasshoppers and grubs in pastures.*

LEFT: *Mangrove forests occur around much of the Australian coastline, even as far south as Melbourne.*

ABOVE: *Male fiddler crabs use their large claw for signalling, cleaning up around the house and attracting a mate. They also use it for fighting the many other males that emerge from their burrows when the tide goes out of the mangroves.*

RIGHT: *Male fiddler crabs staking out their territories.*

LEFT: *The Boobook Owl, named for its call, is common throughout Australia.*
RIGHT: *Tawny Frogmouths spend their days pretending to be tree branches. They fly out at night to feed on insects.*

LEFT: *The Numbat, one of Australia's rarest marsupials, is active during the day and feeds exclusively on termites.*
RIGHT: *Some species of bandicoots inhabit suburban backyards, leaving telltale holes in the lawn as they dig for worms.*

LEFT: *The wood of the Brown Mallet, a eucalypt found in southern Western Australia, was used for mallet handles, and its bark for tannin production.*
RIGHT: *The piping call of the Rufous Treecreeper can be heard in dry woodlands across the south-western part of Australia.*

LEFT: *A skink crawls out of a log.*
RIGHT: *A skink from banksia woodlands of the south-west of Western Australia.*

LEFT: *A praying mantis waits on a leaf for its next prey—perhaps an unsuspecting dragonfly.*

RIGHT: *One of about 300 species of jumping spiders in Australia.*

LEFT: *A Kestrel returns to its nest in the chimney of an old house with a mouse to feed its young. These small falcons are found throughout Australia.*
RIGHT: *A Whistling Kite.*

LEFT: *A various assortment washed up by the sea at Two Peoples Bay, Western Australia.*

RIGHT: *A Sooty Oystercatcher feeds on crustaceans and other sea life. It is found in small numbers around the Australian coastline.*

LEFT: *A Gould's Monitor checks that it's safe to emerge. It came out a moment later carrying a rabbit carcass—they are great scavengers.*

RIGHT: *Some of the Pinnacles at Nambung National Park, Western Australia.*

LEFT: *An aquatic file snake slides across the vegetation floating on a billabong.*
RIGHT: *Paperbark trees cast shadows over an ephemeral freshwater wetland.*

LEFT: *The enormous flowers of the eucalypt known as Mottlecah, a sprawling tree found on the northern sandplains of Western Australia.*
RIGHT: *A male Red-Capped Parrot. This parrot is found only in the south-western corner of Western Australia.*

LEFT: *A Calandrinia plant clings to life in the harsh environment of the Australian mulga.*
RIGHT: *When rains fall in the mulga lands, a profusion of annual plants germinate and flower for a short period of time.*

LEFT: *A small party of Eastern Grey Kangaroos graze in the last of the afternoon light.*
RIGHT: *The Short-beaked Echidna uses its long, sticky tongue to feed mostly on ants and termites.*

LEFT: *Whiskered Terns.*
RIGHT: *The enigmatic Banded Stilt congregates in enormous numbers in hypersaline lakes and wetlands. This is part of a flock of 3000 at the Coorong in South Australia.*

LEFT: *Brightly coloured anemones proliferate in rock pools around the coast.*
ABOVE: *Soldier Crabs marshalling on the estuary floor after the tide has receded.*
RIGHT: *A collection of flotsam and jetsam from a shallow bay.*

LEFT: *Saltwater Crocodiles sit with their mouths open to cool off.*
RIGHT: *Waterways in the north of Australia are home to dangerous Saltwater Crocodiles.*

LEFT: *Sea Lions frolic in the waters off South Australia.*

RIGHT: *Australian Sea Lions frequent isolated bays and sandy beaches of South Australia and southern Western Australia.*

LEFT: *The Western Blue-tongue lizard lives in sandy woodland areas in southern Australia.*
RIGHT: *A Bobtail or Shingleback lizard, from arid southern Australia.*

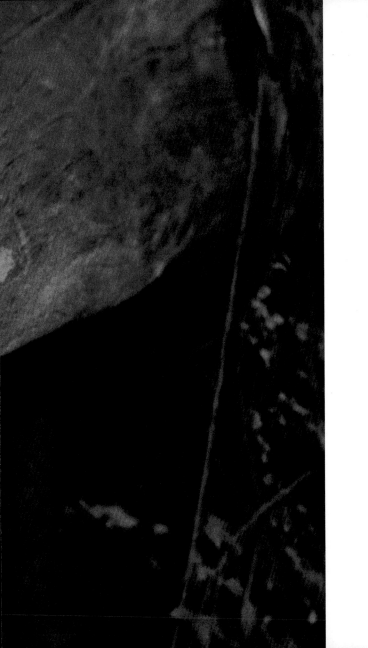

LEFT: *A carpet python, one of Australia's many python species, slides over a log.*

PREVIOUS PAGE: *The comical pelican,*
Victor Harbour, South Australia.
LEFT AND ABOVE: *Eucalypts are highly*
varied in their bark colour and texture.
RIGHT: *Late afternoon sun catches new*
bark on a Jarrah tree, also a eucalypt.

Left: *A brushtail possum carries her baby on her back.*
Right: *A flying fox feeds on wattle flowers.*

LEFT: *The Red-eared Firetail Finch is restricted to wet forests of south-western Australia.*
RIGHT: *The jewel-like Red-winged Wren can be found in the wet forests of south-western Australia.*

LEFT: *Where the rainforest meets the sea—the Daintree Rainforest in northern Queensland.*
RIGHT: *A Ulysses Butterfly, from the rainforests of northern Queensland, here sitting on a frangipani tree in a suburban garden.*

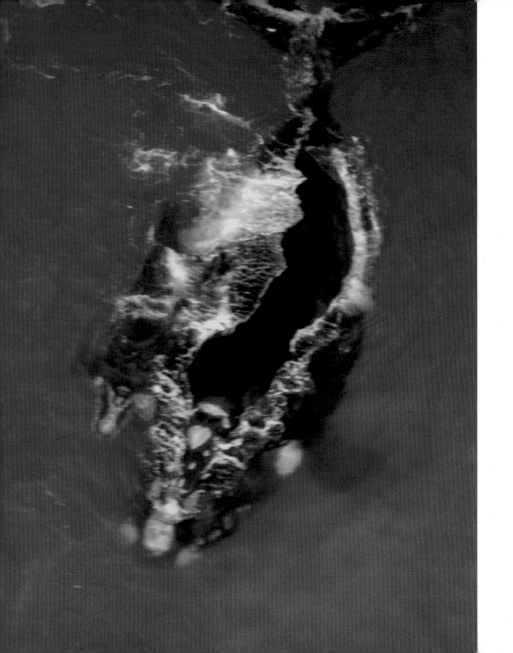

LEFT: *A Humpback Whale with calf.*
RIGHT: *Dolphins are common around the coast of Australia.*

LEFT: *Common Bronzewings coming in to drink at the end of the day. They can be found all over Australia except for far north Queensland.*

RIGHT: *Galahs are common over most of mainland Australia.*

RIGHT: *A wallaby in a snowy Tasmanian landscape.*

LEFT: *One of the many flowering peas to be found in the Jarrah forest of south-western Australia.*

RIGHT: *Ants tending wasp larvae encased in galls.*

LEFT: *Lovely Rainbow Bee-eaters waitng for a meal of dragonflies to come past.*
RIGHT: *A dragonfly successfully captured by a Rainbow Bee-eater.*

LEFT: *Swamp Wallabies live along the east coast, hiding in dense grasses in the forest during the day, and coming out to feed at night.*

RIGHT: *Wombats have powerful limbs and can burrow into even densely packed soil.*

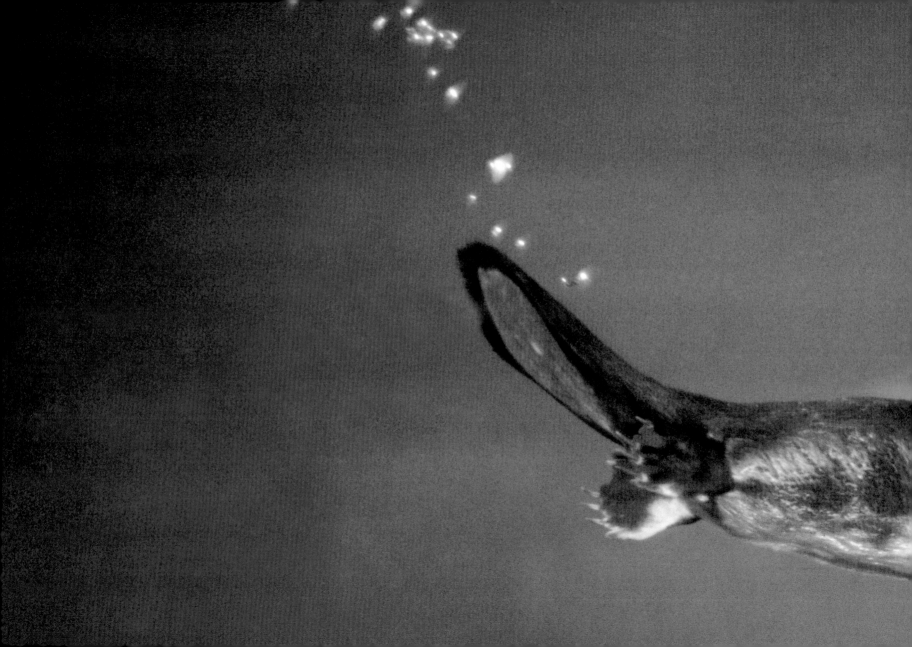

LEFT: *Platypuses dive to the bottom of creeks, where they use their sensitive bills to locate prey in the silt and mud.*

LEFT: *An Emu with chick.*

RIGHT: *Emus often hang around picnic and camping areas, and will eat anything they can get their beaks around, including potato crisp packets.*

NEXT PAGE: *A lone whistling-duck of the far north catches the first rays of the morning sun.*